The British and American Empires and the State of Israel

Until the Kingdom of God comes

Dr. Ali Ansarifar

Dr. Ali Ansarifar

Kingdom Publishers

www.kingdompublishers.co.uk

The British and American Empires and the State of Israel
Until the Kingdom of God comes

Copyright @Ali Ansarifar

All rights reserved. No part of this book may be reproduced in any form by photocopying or any electronic or mechanical means, including information storage or retrieval systems, without permission in writing from both the copyright owner and the publisher of the book. The right of Ali Ansarifar to be identified as the author of this work has been asserted by him in accordance with the Copyright, Designs and Patents Act 1988 and any subsequent amendments thereto.
A catalogue record for this book is available from the British Library.

All Scripture Quotations have been taken from the King James Version of the Bible

ISBN: 978-1-913247-98-0

1st Edition by Kingdom Publishers
Kingdom Publishers
London, UK.

You can purchase copies of this book from any leading bookstore or email contact@kingdompublishers.co.uk

Dr. Ali Ansarifar

Human wisdom searches for the truth diligently.

How can mortality, ignorance and vanity find the truth which has been sealed securely in the beauty and mystery of eternity for a few who take the Yoke of Christ and serve the Holy God for the redemption of mankind?

Man's biggest folly is to think that the truth can be found in religion and religious rituals. How can religious dogmas and belief systems fathom a love which seeks, finds, heals, enlightens, and resurrects one to wholeness in Christ?

Dedication

Those who seek the saving grace of God through Jesus Christ

My wife Amanda

Disclaimer

It has never been the intention of the author of this book to infringe on the sensitivity, personal faith and belief of his readers. The material and information presented in this book have never meant to cause offence to any individual person or to any group of people of any race, creed, nationality and background. This book is written for educational purpose and academic interest only.

Dr. Ali Ansarifar

Preface

Never in the history of mankind the fate of one nation has had such a profound influence on the destiny of all the people in the world. The Bible tells the history of a people, known as Israelites or later as Jews, whom God freed from slavery in Egypt and gave them moral law to make them a model people among the nations. However, their disobedience put them on a path of destruction and brought with it judgement on them and all mankind. The biblical narrative alongside with historical records provide a detailed account of the events leading to a climatic end of the present age, return of Jesus Christ and the beginning of a new age. The return of the Jews to the Holy land in Palestine has been the most significant event in the twenty century and has changed the geopolitical make-up of the Middle East as never before. In this book, the expulsion of the Jews from the Holy land by the Romans and their diaspora will be revisited, and the role that the British and American Empires played in their return to the Holy land will be discussed. The commercial, technological, military, religious, and political conditions which paved the way for the creation of the State of Israel in the Middle East and its eventual rise on the global stage to become the only dominant effective ruling power remaining at the end of the age will be of special interest here. The recent history of the English-speaking people has shown God's providence in action, leading to the birth and growth of the Jewish nation in the Holy land. This has major implications for the fulfilment of the end times biblical prophesies.

Contents

Chapter 1

Expulsion From The Holy Land, Diaspora, Persecution, And Birth Of The Zionist Movement ... 15

Chapter 2

The Rise Of The British Empire - A Divine Providence ... 27

Chapter 3

The Rise Of The American Empire – Israel-United States Relationship And Globalisation ... 41

Chapter 4

The Rise Of A Universal Judaic Empire And End Of The Age ... 53

Chapter 5

Summary And The Coming Of The New Age ... 59

A prayer of thanksgiving ... 65

References ... 67

Epilogue ... 71

Afterword ... 73

Structure of the book

This book consists of the following chapters.

Chapter 1 – The historic events leading to the expulsion of the Jews from the Holy land, their diaspora and subsequent persecution by the Papacy, and the birth of the Zionist movement will be discussed. The Christianisation of the pagan Roman Empire will be re-visited.

Chapter 2 – The rise of the British Empire and its legacy and achievements over the last 300 to 350 years will be examined. The creation of the State of Israel under the British mandate will be of special interest because of its importance in the fulfilment of the biblical promise of the coming Kingdom of God.

Chapter 3 – The historical events which led to the rise of the American Empire and its relationship with the State of Israel will be discussed. The contribution of globalisation to the growth of the State of Israel and the fulfilment of the biblical prophesies of the end times will be discussed.

Chapter 4 – The return of the Jews to Palestine under the British mandate, the building of the third Temple in Jerusalem and the conditions which have been paving the way for the rise of a Universal Judaic Empire and its consequences for mankind at the end of the age will be examined.

Chapter 5 – The role of the American Empire in sustaining the State of Israel will be noted. The final events which will take place in the Holy land in the future will be cited from the Bible prophesies.

Chapter 1
EXPULSION FROM THE HOLY LAND, DIASPORA, PERSECUTION, AND BIRTH OF THE ZIONIST MOVEMENT

The historic events which led to the expulsion of the Jews from the Holy land by the Romans, their diaspora and subsequent persecution by the Papacy, and the birth of the Zionist movement merit further examination. The Christianisation of the pagan Roman Empire was a turning point in the West and had a profound effect on the destiny of the Jews and the gentiles alike.

The ancient Israelites or Israel, also known as Jews, lived in the Holy land in Palestine for centuries before the Roman empire rose to ascendency on the global stage. Two major events shaped the history of the Jews in the pre-Roman period which had a profound effect on their destiny in the post-Roman world. In a lawless period of Israel's history about 1300 BC [1], the Israelites were engaged in military campaigns and military leaders were treated as national heroes by the people. The military leaders were instrumental in the transition in Israel to the monarchy. One of the most famous kings in this period was Solomon the son of king David who ruled over Judah in the south and Israel in the north. Solomon had unusual wisdom, insight and knowledge and composed proverbs and songs. He was immensely rich and had a strong army and during his reign, there was peace and prosperity in the land. Solomon used his wealth and privileges to build a temple in Jerusalem for the worship of the Lord God. After Solomon finished building the Temple in 957 B.C., [2] the Lord's Covenant Box was placed in the Temple and the Tent of the Lord's presence and all its equipment were brought into the Temple. (1 King 8:1-5) The king and all the people dedicated the Temple to the Lord God. God appeared to Solomon and said to him, "If you serve me in honesty and integrity, as your father David did, and if you obey my laws and do everything I have commanded you, I will keep the promise I made to your father David when I told him that Israel would always be ruled by his descendants. But if you and your descendants stop following me, if you disobey the laws and commands I have given you, and worship other gods, then I will remove my people Israel from the land that I have given them. I will also abandon this Temple which I have consecrated as the place where I am to be worshiped. People everywhere will ridicule Israel and treat her with contempt. This Temple will become a pile of ruins and everyone who passes by will be shocked and amazed." (1 King 9:4-8) Soon Solomon's natural instincts and lust for foreign women clouded his best judgments. He married non-Hebrew women even though the Lord had commanded the Israelites not to intermarry with these people, because they would cause Israelites to give their loyalty to other gods. Solomon's wives made him turn away from God and worship foreign gods. Solomon built places of worship where all his foreign wives could burn incense and offer sacrifices to their own gods. This was abomination to the Lord God and He warned Solomon He would take his kingdom away from him. (1 King 11:1-11) After Solomon died, his kingdom fell into civil war and decay and the Northern kingdom came to an end in 722 B.C. The Southern kingdom or the kingdom of Judah was invaded, and Jerusalem was captured by Babylonia in 586 B.C. [3] The Temple in Jerusalem was looted and destroyed, and the high priests and the people of Judah were carried away from their land into exile in Babylonia. Babylonia was then invaded by Cyrus the Great of Persia in 539 B.C., and the exiled Judeans returned to Judah. [4] King Cyrus issued orders for the Temple to be rebuilt. The building of the new Temple was finally completed during the reign of King Darius who ordered all the ornaments to be returned to their proper place in the Jerusalem Temple. Then the people of Israel, the priests and all others who had returned from Babylonia dedicated the Temple to God and the Temple was fully restored in 515 B.C. [5] Soon after the Temple restoration, those who returned from exile brought offerings to be burnt as sacrifices to the God of Israel and worship was resumed. (Ezra 8:35-36) By this time, the Jewish presence in Judah was fully re-established.

The Roman Empire conquered and ruled over a vast land stretching from the Atlantic to the Caspian Sea, and from Britain to the Sahara. In 63 B.C., the province of Judah came under the Roman control. The Romans were very efficient in conquering lands because of their powerful military machine but often faced difficulties in administrating them due to rebellions in their foreign provinces. The rebellion of the Jews was a major challenge to the Roman control over Judah. There were three factors which triggered the revolt: nationalism within the empire;

emperor worship (a pagan religion) and Judaism; and the issue of money. Taxation was a source of income for Rome but who should pay taxes to whom and who should benefit from the protection of being a province within the Empire triggered insurrection in Judah. In fact, the Jews were excluded from Roman citizenship which offered protection and privileges, and experienced discrimination against them. The Jews rioted and clashed with the Roman governor and the army was sent in. Many Jews were killed, and their property confiscated. The first commandment prohibits a Jew from having other Gods before Jehovah. However, the Jews sacrificed to the Divine Roman emperor and the Roman people twice a day as a sign of accommodation with the Romans. Rome needed more money to support its empirical ambitions and heavier taxes were imposed on Judah. Roman soldiers were sent to Jerusalem to collect funds from the Temple treasury and this infuriated the Jews. The tension rose further when the Roman soldiers removed a substantial amount of silver from the Temple treasury. Stealing from the Temple treasury was considered the greatest violation of the Jewish race and its identity. To make the matter worse, soldiers were sent into the most holy of places, violated the sacred objects, and took all the money. The Roman suppression escalated, houses were plundered, and thousands were beaten and killed. As the authority of the local leaders and priests collapsed, nationalism and armed resistance prevailed. This led to more riots and bloody clashes with the Roman soldiers and a full-scale rebellion against the authority of Rome. After some early landmark triumph and outstanding military successes against the might of the Roman army, defeat and disaster ensued. [6]

After some early military set-backs, Rome assembled a large army under Vespasian and his son Titus and invaded Galilee and put to sword its Jewish habitants and combatants and burnt down the town itself and all the surrounding villages. Some Jews committed suicide, and some were sold into slavery. Josephus a Jewish priest and scholar witnessed the slaughter of his people by the Roman army. He believed that God was angry with the Jews and that it was His will that the Romans prosper. After Galilee and the surrounding towns were secured, the Roman army headed for Jerusalem where the Jewish nationalist leaders of the war and the Temple priests were engaged in factional warfare. The moderate religious elites were killed, and the nationalist leaders gained the upper hand, but infighting among the nationalist groups continued with vigour. The Roman army attacked Jerusalem in 70 A.D. and the weakest points in the first wall were bridged and the detachment of the Romans poured in. Soon the soldiers fought their way to the second wall despite stiff resistance from the Jewish fighters but suffered major casualties. As the siege continued, the Jewish population of Jerusalem starved to death and those who wanted to leave the city were killed by their fellow Jews. Some Jews did manage to flee the city secretly at night only to be captured and executed by the Romans, but the Jewish resistance and enthusiasm to wage war did not vain. The Romans built a wall around Jerusalem to prevent anyone from leaving the city and searching for supplies. This weakened the Jewish resistance before a final assault on the city. The Roman strategy worked well, and thousands of Jews starved to death or surrounded to the Romans only to be murdered soon after. The Roman army eventually got through the third wall and despite repeated attempts by the Romans to secure a truce the remaining Jewish fighters refused to surrender. The Romans reached the Temple complex and razed it to the ground and after some days, the Jewish army formations broke down and dispersed. The Jews were slaughtered, and the treasures and ornaments of the Temple were looted and carried off, and what was left of the Temple and its former glory was burnt. The rebellion of the Jews had been crushed and the leaders of the insurgency were hunted down and executed by the Romans. The most humiliating episode in the whole saga was the imposition of the pagan standards into the Temple complex and sacrifices offered to the Roman emperor. The Temple complex in Jerusalem was at the centre of Jewish worship of God and a sure sign of the Jewish identity for centuries. However, its destruction in 70 A.D. ended the main centre of the Jewish presence in the Holy land and began centuries of diaspora and relentless persecution of the Jews for almost two thousand years. [6] As Jesus was leaving the Temple, one of his disciples said, "Look Teacher. What a wonderful stones and buildings." Jesus answered, "You see these great buildings? Not a single stone here will be left in its place; every one of them will be thrown down." (Mark 13:1-2) The Temple in Jerusalem was destroyed, and Jesus's prophetic words were fulfilled. Some years later, a historic event took place in the pagan Western Roman Empire which changed the course of history and had a profound influence on the fate of the Jews in Europe and far beyond for centuries to come.

The event that changed the world – After Jesus was crucified, Christianity grew in the Roman Empire despite intensive and relentless persecution of the early Christian converts. Constantine was the first Christian emperor and the first emperor to sponsor the Christian Church. Christianity thrived throughout the Roman Empire and by 324 A.D. it had become the official religion of the Roman Empire though devotion to the pagan Roman gods had remained with the Roman people. Was Constantine a sincere convert to the Christian God or was he really a self-interested opportunist? Whatever his true intentions were, his decision to support Christianity transformed it into the world religion it is today. [6] The Christianisation of the pagan Roman Empire was a major turning point in the history of the Western Europe and had a huge impact on the lives of the Jews and the destiny of mankind.

The Church became the unifying institution of Constantine's Christian Empire and in 325 A.D., the first universal meeting of the Church took place in the hall of the Palace at Nicaea to resolve some doctrine disputes among the bishops. The council produced the 'Nicene Creed', which is basically an official summary of the Christian faith to this day. Constantine found Jerusalem as a holy city for Christians and Jews and created a new city around the old town of Byzantium, known as Istanbul today, which he named after himself, Constantinople. This was a New Rome located at the strategic point where Europe and Asia meet. After Constantine died, Christianity continued expanding according to the Creed which Constantine left behind. The Christian priesthood and churches grew throughout the Empire and Rome became a major centre for pilgrims. [6] Eventually, the Western and Eastern Christian Churches became dominant forces, ruling over the lives and destiny of millions of people. The Byzantium Empire or Eastern Roman Empire fell to the Ottoman Empire in 1453 A.D. [7] and the Latin Church or the Roman Catholic Church flourished under the rule of the bishops of Rome (the Pops). The Papacy is the office or jurisdiction of the Bishop of Rome, the Pope, and presides over the central government of the Roman Catholic Church. For centuries, the Papacy remained the undisputed ruler of Christendom and most of the world. [8] The Papacy proved to be a potent force on the global stage and its shocking behaviour and excesses are well documented. It has been responsible for nine major religious wars against the Muslims, known as Crusades, (1096-1291 A.D.), and Crusades to eliminate heretics, to create, support and rescue puppet regimes, (1209-1320). The Papacy was also responsible for inquisitions in response to movements considered apostate or heretical to Christianity and to the Papal doctrines (1184-1798). These wars were waged in many countries and regions under the control of the Papal Pontiffs. The most intense and incessant persecution by the Papacy was directed at the Jews, allegedly for killing Christ. These included forced conversion into Christianity, expulsion, desecration accusations, confiscation of property and wealth, imprisonment, slavery, and mass murder. Persecution of the Jews who did not comply to the Roman emperors and their pagan gods was frequent in the pre-Christian era, but it was a lot more targeted, relentless and systematic in the post-Christian era under the Papacy rule [9] and it led to the Holocaust.

Zion is a hill near Jerusalem which widely symbolizes the land of Israel. The Zionist movement advocated establishment of a homeland for the Jewish people in the historic land of Israel in response to centuries of antisemitism, discrimination and persecution. The movement emerged in the late 19th century in Central and Eastern Europe and soon after its birth, its leaders declared creating the desired state in Palestine as their goal. [10]

In the next chapter, the role the British Empire played in creating and developing the State of Israel in the Middle East and the emergence of Israel as the world only major effective ruling power at the end of the age will be discussed.

Chapter 2
THE RISE OF THE BRITISH EMPIRE
- A DIVINE PROVIDENCE

The rise of the British Empire and its contribution to civilisation will be discussed. The legacy of the Empire and the events and achievements of the last 300 to 350 years include, among many, international commerce, industrial revolution and creation of a homeland for the Jews. The latter being of major importance to the fulfilment of the biblical promise of the coming Kingdom of God. God's providence called the British nation to do their historic duty.

The rise and fall of empires throughout history makes interesting stories to tell. Empires rise because men inspire and strive for riches and power and then they collapse into ruins, leaving millions destitute and disillusioned. The circumstances behind the rise of the British Empire and its control and influence over its vast overseas territories and the globe are truly remarkable. It is as the gods of heaven ordained the British nation to be colonisers and conquer the world by Divine providence. Britain being an island was drawn to overseas adventures and expansion and the conquest of foreign lands mainly for its commercial interest. The British Empire is credited for creating the modern world. This was due to the ingenious and industrious nature of its people and their desire to acquire wealth and control the world. Britain is responsible for parliamentary system of government, common law, spread of evangelical protestant Christianity to many millions of pagans, capitalist system for wealth generation, international commerce, scientific and industrial revolutions, banking and finance, sports, outstanding architectures, and modern transport systems. [11] The question is how the modern world steers mankind to its final destiny and fulfils Jesus's promise of the coming Kingdom of God? There must be a final act on the stage of history to close this age and launch a new one. The legacy of the British Empire has been central to this final act of historical importance and the fulfilment of the prophetic words of Jesus.

Territorial expansion, colonisation and international commerce – After some early set-backs in its territorial expansion, Britain had its first break through. The production of Tobacco in the infant colonies of Virginia and Maryland transformed the fortune of both the infant colonies and the British economy and provided Britain with a huge market for domestic consumption and export to the European markets. This made Britain wealthy and its power grew and set the scene for the further colonisation of North America which was fertile and rich in natural resources. Britain was then drawn to the Caribbean where in Barbados sugar was produced and exported. This was followed by the very lucrative slave trade which replaced the reluctant and scarce imported European labourers with negroes from Africa. The British sugar plantation owners became very rich and as the domestic market and European market grew, the British economy benefited greatly. This encouraged further incursion and colonisation of other islands. In 1600 AD, the international trade took a major turning. Britain formed the London-based East India Company to by-pass the middlemen in the eastern Mediterranean and deal with spice suppliers in the East Indies directly. This was a successful enterprise and made the Company very rich and then Company set up new factories on the Indian coast. The competition with other powers forced Britain to adopt a more aggressive stand against Portuguese and Dutch and established new trading posts along the western and eastern shores of the

Indian subcontinent. British manufactured goods were exported, and Indian goods were imported. The Company created shipping business which carried goods between India and Arabian ports and the Far East. As the commerce expanded, variety of goods were exported to Britain from India and more ships visited the ports in Arabia, Persia and China with British manufactured goods. Textiles produced in India were imported into Britain and then re-exported to Europe and West Africa to exchange for slaves. [12] Some nations embraced international trade with Briton and some were not so keen. A trade war was developed between Britain and China in the 18th century when China was enjoying a good trade balance with Europe. Britain cultivated opium in India and exported it to China. But China reacted by making opium illegal. This made the matter worse and America joined in with Briton to enforce a stricter regime of opium smuggling into China. Opium continued pouring into China in vast quantities until 1834 A.D. when the trade ceased. However, Briton used a military force against the Chines to recover financial losses of the British traders and to secure new security for trade. China was defeated and surrounded the Hong Kong Island as well as five treaty ports to Briton. Furthermore,

China paid a huge sum of money to both Briton and France and granted them most favoured nations status. The opium wars continued to engulf China for many more years, forcing China to make major concessions to foreign powers. In the final act of humiliation, China signed a treaty in 1858, which paid reparations for the expenses of the wars, legalised the opium trade, and gave rights to foreign traders and missionaries to travel within China. [13] This was a clear signal to the Chinese and other nations that international trade was here to stay, and we were all a part of this new global phenomenon whether we like it or not.

The British trade expanded as more people emigrated mostly to the colonies in North America. The new emigrants were dependent on new home-manufactured goods which had to be transported from Britain and Caribbean to North America across the Atlantic. The profitable transatlantic trade was born. The creation of Commonwealth in 1649 was a major boast to Trade for Britain. It expanded the British Overseas Territories and the trade and enhanced the British influence over all aspects of commerce. The wealth generated from trade helped the British navy to re-arm and challenge powerful Spanish, Portuguese and Dutch navies. Soon the British fleet expanded in number and size and became a national force to protect the trade routes and commercial interests of Britain all over the world. This vast naval power also helped Britain to secure more precious territories in Jamaica, St Helena and Gibraltar and added them to its chest of treasure. By 1922, more than 1/5 of the world's population lived in the British Empire and Britain controlled almost ¼ of the Earth's total land area. The Empire had reached the pinnacle of its power, wealth, prestige and influence on the global stage and was the largest Empire the world has ever seen. The African slave trade was at the core of this incredible success as it was the case with other European colonial powers. But Britain was the first of the European powers to abolish slavery. [14] It is amazing how the lives and destiny of millions of people almost in every continent changed forever by a nation who thought they were destined to be colonisers and conquer the world. This coupled with an incredible appetite for procurement of wealth set the scene for international commerce.

Scientific and Industrial revolutions and the birth of the modern age

In the history of great civilisations, a period from 1598 to 1715, known as the Golden Century, is probably the most momentous time in the rise of the Western civilisation. In fact, the modern world started in the 17th century. The invention of printing, the mariner's compass, microscope, telescope, thermometer, barometer and pendulum clock, and the rise of modern science such as astronomy, mathematics and physics started the ball rolling. The revolutionary idea of the time emphasised the importance of investigating the corporal world and taking nothing for granted. It was believed that a view of the natural world could be formed after many experiments were performed and generalisation had to be based upon workable hypothesis. For the first time, knowledge could be gained by rational and experimental methods. This laid the foundation of empiricism and modern science and was the beginning of the European enlightenment which gradually eroded traditional Christianity. The seventeenth century was the age of science and the eighteenth century the age of reason. During this period, scientific methods were being applied more rigorously to astronomy, chemistry, biology, zoology, history, biblical criticism, politics and economics. This astonishing outburst of scientific progress in the latter half of the seventeenth century took place in Protestant countries and England played a leading role. [15] The enlightenment shaped other fields of intellectual endeavours such as epistemology and psychology, religion, optimism and the problem of evil, political theories, and progress and history. [16]

In a period from 1760 to 70, Britain took a giant leap forward in innovations in arts, science and industry. It invented machinery for making commodities such as cotton, iron, steel and pottery. Probably, the invention of steam engines was by far the most important step in modernising transportation and accelerating movement of people and commodities. This was the beginning of the manufacturing industry or industrialisation. Expansion in manufacturing capacity and technical know-how reinforced the British naval capabilities and Britain ruled the waves unchallenged. The industrial Revolution proceeded slowly but was almost complete by 1860. Britain's international trading position made it the workshop of the world in the eighteenth century. The wealth accumulated from both industry and agriculture, referred to as capital, were exported into foreign and imperial investments. With the industrial revolution came also a financial revolution which made Britain empire of money and by 1870, Britain became the world moneylender and exporter of capital. The capitalist system for wealth generation and distribution was born. This enabled Britain to develop other economies and stimulated more demands which in turn helped the international trade. However, uninterrupted passage of goods and services through nations and local legal systems was a prerequisite for free trade. This could only be achieved if local legal systems guaranteed justice to the businessmen who sustained losses. [12] This warranted laws to secure trade and Britain was instrumental in forging the international law to safeguard trade (1800 to 1850). [17]

A revolution in communication which facilitated long-distance travel and wireless had a huge effect on the running of the Empire in the first half of the nineteenth century. Aviation was at the core of this revolution with the British aircraft manufacturing booming in the period before and during the first world-war. Highly skilled British aviators flew all over the territories in the Empire and continents and soon imperial civil aviation was established and by 1932 there were regular flights between some cities in the Empire. The age of international civil passenger air travel began in 1938, opening affordable travel to thousands of people within the Empire and world-wide. Like air travel, the wireless draw people together and improved the Britain's ability to educate people of different races and creeds in its domain to learn about the benefits of the Empire. The cinema played even a bigger role in both entertaining and educating the masses. It was around 1926 and 1930 when the power of cinema and films became apparent to the administrators of the Empire by way of enhancing cohesion among its subjects and the film industry came into existence. [12] By 1930, international free trade and capitalism, industrial manufacturing, air travel, rapid communication by wireless, and cinema and film industry were added to mankind's list of achievements. These technological advances improved the education of millions of people and provided entertainment for them.

The British mandate in Palestine and the Balfour declaration – The land of Palestine was under the Ottoman control for 400 years and was handed over to the British in 1918 after the collapse of the Ottoman Empire at the end of the first World War. [18] The British administration of Palestine, referred to as British mandate, was in force from 1923 to 1948. The purpose of the mandate was to provide administrative support for the territory until its indigenous people could take full control and run their affairs normally. The Balfour Declaration of 1917, which was fully supported by the Zionist movement, pledged a future national homeland for the Jews alongside the Palestinian Arabs in Palestine. Under the terms of the Balfour Declaration, Britain welcomed Jewish immigrations into Palestine. By doing so, Britain allied itself with the international Zionist movement, paving the way for the creation of the State of Israel. [12] The 30 years of the British control of Palestine was marred with riots and constant conflict between its Arab and Jewish populations, leading to nationalism and conflict on both sides. As the British mandate came to an end, the Jews who returned to the Holy land from diaspora declared independence and the State of Israel came into existence officially in 1948. [19] This changed the geopolitical complexion of the Middle East in a way which nobody could have envisaged and triggered a permanent state of conflict between the Muslims and the Jewish State to this day with Jerusalem being the main area of contention.

The British Empire has left many legacies behind among which the Industrial revolution, the capitalist system of wealth generation and distribution, international commerce and the creation of the State of Israel in the Middle East are probably the most important of all. The industrial revolution created the modern technological age, capitalism, and international commerce shaped the current class structure, and establishment of the State of Israel has instigated one of the biggest conflicts in the modern history of the Middle East. The technological advances of recent years have led to the development of a digital age and use of artificial intelligent (AI) and robotics, the capitalist system has led to an unprecedented wealth disparity, and the presence of the State of Israel in the Holy land has fixated our attention on the prophetic words of the end times in the Bible. It is as some benevolent force in the universe selected the British Empire to be the bearer of the seed of the State of Israel until the seed became embryonic and an infant (Israel) was born. The American Empire which proceeded the British Empire would take the infant to its full adulthood to accomplish its pre-determined historic mission.

In the next chapter, the rise of the American Empire and its steadfast support for the State of Israel will be discussed. One wonders if there was a Divine providence in all these events.

Chapter 3
THE RISE OF THE AMERICAN EMPIRE – ISRAEL-UNITED STATES RELATIONSHIP AND GLOBALISATION

The historic events leading to the rise of the American Empire and its relationship with the State of Israel in the Middle East will be discussed. There will be a short note on globalisation and its role in the fulfilment of the biblical prophesies of the end times.

The origin of America - The colonists in North America who were mostly of British descent, referred to as the Americans, were considered sons of the mother country England and were expected to share all the legal and political rights of their brothers and sisters in Britain. However, the Americans, who were patriotic by nature and proud of their connection with Britain, were dismayed by the fact that they were excluded from the constitutional rights and liberties which were granted to Britons, despite being part of an empire which in principle granted liberty and security to its subjects. At the same time, the American society was learning to avoid aristocracy, which was a whole mark of the British society, and it was the talent and labour rather than birth that paved the way for a man's success. The American temperament was evolving to become less submissive unquestioningly to authority, and the Americans avoided paying taxes and duties on imported goods. Britain resorted to deploying military forces to deal with unrest and non-compliance, but this made the matter worse and stiffened the resolve of the dissident colonists whose number increased substantially. Meanwhile, the British political elite were deeply concerned with the rise of liberal ideas in America and decided to adopt a policy that transformed civil protests into an armed conflict. Britain allocated a great chunk of territory which normally was opened to the Americans for settlement to Canada, and recognised Catholicism as the official religion of Canada. The America population at that time was mainly Protestant and was alarmed by this event and put in place a series of economic measures to boycott all trade with Britain and its other colonies and started arming itself. [12]

By the end of 1774. The British power in North America was weakening and Americans were gaining more freedom. Although the hard-liners in America were keen to avoid military conflict with Britain by offering concessions, the

British government refused to compromise. This led to military clashes and guerrilla war fare and Britain was forced to assemble an army for a war with the Americans. The British military campaign was successful at its early stages but in 1776 the radicals in the American camp secured a Declaration of Independence which destroyed all political and constitutional links with Britain. By 1777, there were signs that the American republic was going to survive, and the British military was facing defeat. As the British military campaign disintegrated, the American dream of freedom from the British rule became a reality. However, the Angelo-American trade grew massively and the British view that colonies were exclusive markets, protected and controlled in the economic interest of the mother country fell apart. Instead, the concept of Free Market was proposed which declared, "A product of natural human competition, which, if unfettered by official rules and unhindered by monopolies, provided the most efficient distribution of resources and the greatest benefits to the consumer." [12] State control over their trade, i.e. through regulations, had to be avoided because it would handicap commerce and interfere with natural market forces and prices. This idea undermined the economic arguments which justified the empire and reinforced effort towards international free market. Anyhow, Britain over stretched its naval and military resources and capabilities by the territories which it conquered by 1762 and its decline was inevitable. [12]

The British intransigence to the American inspiration for freedom and equal right set the scene for the American war of independence and in 1776 Declaration of Independence was finally passed. [12] The independent movement was supported by the French through various treaties in 1778 and in return the French guaranteed the American Independence. The British resolve to continue military campaign in North America was exhausted after very costly military engagements with Spain and France. Britain finally agreed to withdraw its troops from the North American garrisons and a treaty was signed between Britain and America in 1783, granting full independence to the Americans. A new independent English-speaking nation came into existence on the continent of North America for the first time. [20] In the late 18th century, America expanded massively and by 1848, it covered the continent. Major international military conflicts abroad such as World Wars 1 and 2 established America or the

United States as a world power. The American military, economic, technological might and global reach made it the World's only superpower after the collapse of the Soviet Union in 1991. The political system of America is based on representative democracy which many nations have been inspired to emulate in the running of their internal affairs and policies for many years. The constitution of America or its supreme law came into force in 1789. One unique feature of the constitution is the Bill of Rights which offers protections of individual liberty and justice and limits the powers of government. [21]

Relationship between Israel and the United States – The mutual relationship between Israel and the United States began in 1960. The United State has been the strongest supporter of Israel and vital to its internal stability and external security by providing military, economic, financial and diplomatic assistance. In fact, this relationship has been pivotal to the overall American foreign policy in the Middle East region for the last 70 years, so much so that Israel today is the largest annual recipient of American aid with military assistance being the largest component of the package. Israel is now a major trade partner with the United States and has been protected from various resolutions by the American veto power in the United Nations Security Council. The relationship between the United States and Israel has come a long way since 1948 when America showed sympathy for the creation of the Jewish state to full dependence on the United States for its ultimate survival. It is inconceivable that Israel could survive a regional or global military conflict without immediate and direct assistance from the United States. [22] There is no doubt that the relationship with America has been incredibly beneficial to the growth and maturity of the State of Israel since its creation, and it will continue to be so until a global Judaic Empire rises in the Middle East with its capital in Jerusalem. However, before Israel emerges on the global stage as the only remaining major power, certain conditions must prevail with globalisation being at the heart of this universal transformation.

A biblical perspective on the past events - After the Noah's flood, the children of men were ungodly. They assembled and built a city and a very high and strong tower in the land they inhabited so that they could rise into heaven. In those days, King Nimrod ruled securely over all the earth, and all the earth became one people, speaking one tongue and uniform words. They made fame for themselves and reigned upon the entire world, and they were secured from their enemies within their borders. However, the building of the tower was a transgression and a sin against the Lord God of heaven because they in their hearts waged war against Him and wanted to go up into heaven. After the city and the tower were built, all the people and families were divided into three parts. One part wanted to ascend to heaven and fight against God, one part wanted to ascend to heaven to place their own gods and serve them, and one part wanted to ascend to heaven and strike God with bows and spears. As men's hostility towards God grew, they casted the arrows towards heaven. The Lord God and His holy angles came down and confused their language, so people could no longer understand one another's speech and disagreed. The part who wanted to ascend to heaven to fight against God was dispersed throughout the earth and the remaining two parts were destroyed by God. The people who were left turned away from building the city and the tower. The place where the Lord confused the language of the whole earth, is called Babel. Later, the Lord destroyed the tower and many people died in that tower. In fact, Babel is the place where people were dispersed into cities and nations with different languages and customs and co-existed in disharmony to this day. [23] Centuries of warfare among the nations has prevented strong and very tall towers from rising and whenever they did, they were destroyed by the ferocity of human conflict. The Lord God has kept the vanity of the ungodly man in check by infighting among them until the day of judgment. Whilst the righteous man travels on a straight and narrow path to salvation and eternal life with the hope of redemption in Christ, the unrighteous man journeys on a path of never-ending conflict to its self-destruction and ultimately damnation in hell. It is worth remembering that we are the descendants of those men who wanted to ascend to heaven to fight against God. In fact, we have never ceased waging war against God on so many facades. For example, in the modern age, Darwinism, atheistic Marxism, and secular science have been the most widely used disciplines for questioning or denying the existence of God altogether. It is prudent to take heed of the fate of those who came before us and perished, not knowing the truth. Human wisdom searches for the truth diligently. How can mortality, ignorance and vanity find the truth which has been sealed securely in the beauty and mystery of eternity for a few who take the Yoke of Christ and serve the Holy God for the redemption of mankind?

Globalisation and the future of mankind - The term globalisation, which appeared in the 1960s, is used extensively in academia and media but there is no clear definition of what it means and at times, it remains an abstract concept. There are so many definitions for globalisation so let us take one definition which says, "globalisation refers to a set of social processes that are thought to transform our present social condition into one of globality." [24] At the heart of globalisation lies changing forms of human contact and movement towards greater interdependence and integration. The term "globality" is important to understand because it has a biblical connotation to it as will be discussed later. But first, let's consider briefly how globalisation can be accomplished. [24]

The process by which globalisation can be achieved is complex and demanding. The advocates of globalisation believe that the traditional political, economic, cultural, and geographical boundaries must be eradicated. This can be achieved by creating of new and the multiplication of existing social networks and activities. The combination of professional networking, technological innovation, and political decisions can create new social orders. The social relations, activities, and interdependencies must be expanded and stretched and moreover, the social exchange and activities must be intensified and accelerated. The globalisation process must educate people to become conscious of increasing social interdependence and the acceleration of social interactions. Once people are aware of the diminishing national boundaries and distances, they will embrace a global whole and their individual and collective identities will change and behave differently in the world. A wide range of technological innovations and advanced technologies are available to meet these ambiguous targets. For example, satellites, financial markets, electronic trading, huge shopping malls, and internet are integral parts of this universal transformation. There are economic, political, cultural, and ideological dimensions to globalisation. Since the end of the second world war, three major international economic organisations have been created to reinforce and support globalisation. They are the International Monetary Fund, the International Bank or World Bank, and the World Trade Organisation. Moreover, there has been a major boost to internationalised trade and finance. On the political front, some argue that accelerated techno-economic forces have made politics powerless and governmental ability to introduce restrictive policies and regulations are consequently grossly hampered. As a result, globalisation erodes nation-state, and nation-states will have no effective control because of the discipline imposed by economic choices made elsewhere. It is increasingly evident that in globalisation there is no place for nation-states and regional clubs and agencies will eventually replace the nation-states as the basic unit of governance. Culture is yet another domain of human experience which has not escaped the influence of globalisation. The fundamental question is whether globalisation makes people more similar or more different. It is argued that globalisation imposes uniform standards across the world and this will hinder human creativity and destroy social relations. This will be very harmful to human cultural advancement. Additionally, there has been a shift in the global use of language where some languages are used in international communication more widely while others lose their importance and disappear because less people speak them. Today more than 80% of the material posted on the internet is in English and almost 50% of the international students are studying in English-speaking countries. All the indications are that the English language will be used globally in the future and many other languages will either disappear or their use will be marginalised. [24]

It is as we have gone around a circle and soon all mankind will literary live in a global village. Globalisation is paving the way for all the nations in the world to become one people once again, speaking one tongue and uniform words as it was at the time of King Nimrod in Babel.

In the next chapter, some biblical verses will be used to discuss how globalisation is preparing the State of Israel to rise as a major power in the Middle East to rule the world in accordance with the prophesies of the end times.

Chapter 4
THE RISE OF A UNIVERSAL JUDAIC EMPIRE AND END OF THE AGE

The return of the Jews to Palestine under the British mandate and the building of the third Temple in Jerusalem will be discussed in the light of the prophesies in the Bible. The conditions which are helping the rise of a Universal Judaic Empire and its consequences for mankind at the end of the age will be examined.

Return to the Holy land and the building of the third Temple – The State of Israel was established in 1948 after millions of Jews were exterminated during the Holocaust and the residing minorities in different nations were repatriated and some emigrated voluntarily to their historic homeland after centuries of diaspora. Meanwhile, the Jewish State has provided a place where Jews became a majority nation in their own state, but the indigenous Palestinians were exiled and became refuges in other countries to this day. Since its creation, the Jewish State had to address numerous threats to its continued existence and security but has managed to defeat its enemies and grown in military power and stature. [10]

There are numerous prophesies in the Bible regarding the return of the Jews to the Holy land. "Yes, I say, you will find me, and I will restore you to your land. I will gather you from every country and from every place to which I have scattered you, and I will bring you back to the land from which I had sent you away into exile. I, the Lord, have spoken." (Jeremiah 29:4). The Jews in diaspora longed to return to the Holy land for centuries. They probably assumed and expected that the Holy God shared their longing for return to the Holy land equally. The verses in the Bible were written to reflect God's willingness to restore the place back to the Jews who were promised the land in the ancient past. But this is unlikely since their presence in the Holy land for millennia was fruitless and highly problematic as the destruction of the first and second Temples in Jerusalem by the Babylonians and Romans, respectively, and their subsequent diaspora and slavery in the foreign lands had indicated. It is inconceivable that an omnipotent and omniscient Holy God would unleash a bloody Holocaust on "His own People" to facilitate their return to the Holy land. But it is feasible that these biblical verses were added by the scribes, sometime after the destruction of the Temple in Jerusalem and expulsion from the Holy land, who hoped that sometime in the future the Bible believers would sympathise with their predicament and eventually grant the Jews the right of return to the Holy land, supposedly fulfilling God's aspiration for His people. Indeed, this is what happened over seventy years ago under the British mandate in Palestine. Since it was established, the State of Israel has benefitted greatly from the moral and financial supports of the Zionist Christians. The Zionist Christians living in the English-speaking countries particularly in the United States and Britain supported the creation of a homeland for the Jews and have been and continue to be highly supportive of the State of Israel. [25]

The Jewish presence in the Holy land has always been intertwined with building a temple in Jerusalem, which has been the centre of Jewish religious rituals, worship and identity for millennia. There is a secret plan to build a third Temple with a view to accelerate the coming of Messiah. However, there are gruesome prophesies in the Bible about the unfolding future events in Jerusalem when a third Temple will be built. "He will oppose every so-called god or object of worship and will put himself above them all. He will even go in and sit down in God's Temple and claim to be God." (2Thess: 2:4) "You will see the awful horror of which the prophet Daniel spoke. It will be standing in the Holy place. Then those who are in Judea must run away to the hills." (Matt 24:15-16) There are some organisations in Israel today which are responsible for preparing the third Temple and restoring sacrificial worship. It is believed that the restoration of the third Temple will bring back the light into the world which was present when the Lord was in the Temple and will enable humanity to rise to its greatest potential through its relationship with God. All ornaments and musical instruments required for performing religious rituals and duties are crafted and a priesthood is being trained to perform the Temple duties. Even a Red Heifer is being bred to be sacrificed in the ritual purification of the priests but the land on which the Temple is to be built is not yet prepared. There are major disputes and at times outbreak of violence between the Muslims and Jews regarding the status of the Temple Mount. [26] Major archaeological work is being carried out in Israel nowadays and sooner or later, the original foundation of the second Temple will be discovered, and the construction of the third Temple will begin in earnest. This will bring peace between the Jews and Muslims and resolve the conflict on the Temple Mount. However, according to the prophesies in the Bible, the peace will be short lived and when the son of sin or antichrist sits in the Temple and claims to be God, all the hell will break loss. Before we get to this final act and the end of the age, the Babel must rise again, and the King of Babel must control and rule over all mankind.

As we leave the industrial age (legacy of the British Empire) behind and enter the information or digital age (legacy of the American Empire), there are unprecedented changes coming which will affect our lives in a way that could not have been foreseen. Artificial intelligent (AI), robotics, and electronic banking, transactions and trade are at the forefront of this revolution. AI is human-like intelligent exhibited by a machine, for example a computer or a robot. It combines various capabilities such as recognising objects, understanding and responding to language, making decision, and solving problems to perform specific functions which normally humans perform. [27] Electronic banking, also known as electronic funds transfer, is the use of electronic means to transfer funds, which is in digital form, directly from one account to another at the speed of light. [28] These modern platforms, which are highly centralised, give King Babel ability to know details of our personal lives and to control all aspects of our finances. For example, if King Babel does not approve of somebody's Christian credentials, he may just terminate his/her bank account at the touch of a button. Imagine if King Babel is the antichrist who is obsessed with getting men to worship him and will use any means to achieve it. Then the Devil took Jesus to a very high mountain and showed him all the kingdoms of the world in all their greatness. "All this I will give you," the Devil said, "If you kneel down and worship me." Then Jesus answered, "Go away, Satan." (Matt 4: 8-9) Jesus managed to resist the Devil, but will we be able to do the same thing and not worship the beast if we cannot buy and sell? The Apostle Paul said, "Build up your strength in union with the Lord and by means of His mighty power. Put on all the armour that God gives you, so that you will be able to stand up against the Devil's evil tricks. Then when the evil day comes, you will be able to resist the enemy's attacks; and after fighting to the end, you will still hold your ground." (Eph 6:10-13) In Christ, we will prevail against the man of sin and his wiles and receive the crown of glory.

Chapter 5
SUMMARY AND THE COMING OF THE NEW AGE

A brief note on the metamorphosis of the State of Israel in the British Empire until its birth in the Middle East will be written. The role of the American Empire in sustaining the newly created State of Israel will be noted. The final events which will take place in the Holy land will be cited from the prophesies in the Bible

The term "metamorphosis" means transformation. It is one of the most fascinating life changing processes in nature. One good example is a butterfly which goes through four different stages of metamorphosis. Firstly, the butterfly lays its small eggs on the leaves of the host plant. After a week or two, the eggs hatch. The larva develops inside the egg and nourishes on the yolk of the egg. Then, they make a small hole in the egg and emerge on the leaf. Secondly, the larva or caterpillar eats its own egg shell and then the leaves of the host plant to nourish itself. The adult caterpillar starts to shed its skins and then crawls away from the host plant until it finds a safe-haven to develop into an insect in the development stages between larva and adult. Thirdly, the caterpillar slowly transforms itself in the development stages between larva and adult to form a butterfly. In the fourth and final stage, the caterpillar radically converts itself into a beautiful butterfly and gets ready to fly. However, the butterfly is still weak and cannot fly until a life-saving fluid is pumped into its body to enable it to fly. [29]

The story of the creation of the State of Israel has a similar connotation to the metamorphosis of a butterfly. The British Empire was the host, the egg laid on the host was the idea behind the creation of a Jewish State in Palestine proposed by the Zionist lobby and fully endorsed by the Zionist Christians, and the small hole in the egg was the Balfour Declaration. Once the idea of creating a Jewish State and right of return were fully entrenched in the host by the Zionist movement, it gained momentum and using the very resources of the host, the new State shed its chains and crawled away from the clutches of the British mandate and found a safe-haven in its own territorial boundary in Palestine. Like a freshly converted butterfly from a caterpillar, it was still weak and could not fully stand on its own feet until life-saving economic, financial, and military technology aids coupled with diplomatic support were pumped into its body. The State of Israel has been supported by the American Empire since its beginning and as the American Empire declines and losses its prestige and dominance on the global stage, a powerful and highly advanced State of Israel will emerge unexpectedly from behind the curtains to rule the world for the last time. Recall in metamorphosis, the host must die first before the new creature emerges. On this basis, the American Empire must die first before the State of Israel rises to replace it. This is what is happening now. The Israeli State will possess the most sophisticated military technology, AI, international electronic banking, transaction and trade platforms, and extraordinary power of the mass media (all legacies of the British and American Empires). No empire in history has ever had such impressive range of capabilities and benefits of the scientific and technological advances at its disposal to control and rule over its citizens and ultimately the entire world. This will be a Universal Judaic Empire, the home of the third Temple in Jerusalem where according to the Bible prophesies the antichrist will sit in and claim to be God. (2Thess 2:3-4) The unfolding future events in Jerusalem will adversely affect all the nations and mesmerise people, like a colourful butterfly to an observer. However, before a Universal Judaic Empire emerges on the global stage as the only ruling power, some shocking events must take place both in the Middle East and world-wide.

"There will be strange things happening to the sun, the moon, and the stars. On earth whole countries will be in despair, afraid of the roar of the sea and the raging tides. People will faint from fear as they wait for what is coming over the whole earth for the powers in space will be driven from their courses." (Luke 21:25-27) "And don't be troubled when you hear the noise of battles close by and news of battles far away. Such things must happen, but they do not mean that the end has come. Countries will fight each other; kingdoms will attack one another. There will be earthquakes everywhere, and there will be famine. These things are like the first pains of Child birth." (Mark 13:7-9) We are now entering a critical phase in human history where the first pains of child birth are showing up everywhere. There is sever moral decay, economic and financial collapse, military conflicts and lawlessness, civil unrest, breakdown of family values, explosion of false religions and gospels, corruption and dishonesty, persecution of Christians, and rejection of God and His moral law world-wide. This can only lead to total anarchy and break down of all civilised rules and norms before the coming of antichrist. So, let us remember what Jesus said. "To those who win the victory, I will give some of the hidden manna. I will also give each of them a white stone on which is written a new name that no one knows except the one who receives it." (Revelation 2:17) "Those who win the victory will be clothed like this in white, and I will not remove their names from the book of the living. In the presence of my Father in heaven and of His angels I will declare openly that they belong to me." (Revelation 3:5) The Lord by His mercy will take those who abide in Christ the Saviour faithfully through the difficult days ahead. We must remain in the Lord with courage, love and hope for the coming turbulent days. It is a wonder that the Divine providence raised the British and American Empires to rule the world to create the modern age. Even more so, it is wonder of all wonders that the Bible prophesies laid the seed of the State of Israel in the wombs of these Empires to be born, nourished and then raised to govern the world at the end of the age. The final act in the third Temple in Jerusalem will be the climax of this astonishing chapter of mankind's history. We must take heed not to be deceived and always remember the words of our Lord Jesus Christ, "Do not let anyone deceive you in any way. For the Day will not come until the final rebellion takes place and the Wicked one appears, who is destined to hell." (2Thess: 3)

Centuries of warfare and bloodshed will soon end, and God's King, Jesus Christ, will rule over mankind in peace and justice. Praise the name of the Almighty Lord God for His mercy on the righteous.

A PRAYER OF THANKSGIVING

I thank thee o Lord God:

for the gift of faith;

for your faithfulness and abundant mercy;

for giving sight to see and granting wisdom to understand the scriptures;

for Jesus Christ the Saviour who washes feet, cleanses heart and gives hope of eternal life;

for the Saviour who gives such words and wisdom that no enemy will be able to refute or contradict;

for the purity of heart and clarity of mind through Jesus Christ the Saviour;

for calling to service to seek, find, save and redeem those who suffer injustice, prejudice, and assault on their dignities;

for granting peace to sincere hearts to share a prayer with Jesus;

"Our Father in heaven:
may your holy name be honoured;
may your kingdom come;
may your will be done on earth as it is in heaven.
Give us today the food we need.
Forgive us the wrongs we have done as we forgive the wrongs that others have done to us.
Do not bring us to hard testing and keep us safe from the Evil One."

(Matt 6:9-13)

REFERENCES

1. https://www.booksofthebible.net/the-book-of-judges#:~:text=Written%20around%201000%20BC%2C%20the%20book%20of%20Judges,300%20years%20going%20back%20to%20around%201300%20BC. Date visited: 01/11/2019

2. https://www.britannica.com/topic/Temple-of-Jerusalem Date visited: 03/11/2020

3. Good News Bible, Today's English Version, The Bible Societies, Collins/Fontana, 1976.
(ISBN: 0564 003018 for the Bible Society)
(ISBN: 0005126215 for the Collins)

4. https://en.wikipedia.org/wiki/Babylonian_captivity date visited: 03/11/2020

5. https://www.historyandheadlines.com/history-november-21-164-bc-second-temple-dedicated-jerusalem-origin-hanukkah/ Date visited: 04/11/2020

6. Simon Baker, Ancient Rome, The Rise and Fall of an Empire, BBC Books, an imprint of Ebury Publishing, A Random House Group Company, 2007.
(ISBN: 978 1 846 07284 0)

7. https://en.wikipedia.org/wiki/Byzantine_Empire
   Date visited: 07/11/2020

8. https://www.britannica.com/topic/papacy
   Date visited: 07/11/2020

9. Ray Montgomery, Bob O'Dell, the List, Persecution of Jews by Christians throughout history, Root Source Press, Israel, 2019. (ISBN: 978-965-7738-13-9)

10. https://en.wikipedia.org/wiki/Zionism
    Date visited: 07/11/2020

11. https://en.wikipedia.org/wiki/British_Empire
    Date visited: 08/12/2020

12. Lawrence James, The Rise and Fall of the British Empire, Abacus Publishers, London, 1998. (ISBN 978-0-349-10667-0)

13. https://en.wikipedia.org/wiki/Opium_Wars
    Date visited: 12/12/2020

14. https://simple.wikipedia.org/wiki/British_Empire
    Date visited: 14/12/2020

15. Maurice Ashley, The Golden Century, Europe 1598-1715, CARDINAL, Sphere Books Ltd, London, 1975. (ISBN o 351 15152 4)

16. J. F. Lively, Problems and Perspectives in History, The Enlightenment, Longmans Green and Co Ltd, London, 1966.

17. https://core.ac.uk/download/pdf/232640381.pdf
Date visited: 16/12/2020

18. https://www.dailysabah.com/feature/2018/05/18/400-years-of-peace- Palestine-under-ottoman-rule
Date visited: 16/12/2020

19. https://en.wikipedia.org/wiki/Mandate_for_Palestine
Date visited: 18/12/2020

20. https://en.wikipedia.org/wiki/American_Revolutionary_War   Date visited: 24/12/2020

21. https://en.wikipedia.org/wiki/United_States
Date visited: 25/12/2020

22. https://en.wikipedia.org/wiki/Israel%E2%80%93United_States_relations
Date visited: 25/12/2020

23. Joseph B. Lumpkin, The books of Enoch, The angles, the watchers and the Nephilim, Fifth Estate Publishers USA, 2011. (ISBN: 9781936533077)

24. Manfred B. Steger, Globalization, A very short introduction, Oxford University Press, Oxford, 2003. (ISBN: 0-19-280359-X-79108)

25. https://en.wikipedia.org/wiki/Christian_Zionism
Date visited: 28/12/2020

26. https://free.messianicbible.com/feature/end-time-prophecy-why-is-the-third-temple-so-important/
Date visited: 29/12/2020

27. https://www.ibm.com/cloud/learn/what-is-artificial-intelligence   Date visited: 29/12/2020

28. http://sjecnotes.weebly.com/uploads/5/2/5/1/5251788/26494919-definition-of-e-banking.pdf   Date visited: 29/12/2020

29. https://animalsake.com/butterfly-metamorphosis
date visited: 30/12/2020

All the verses cited in this book were taken from the Good News Bible, Today's English Version, The Bible Societies, Collins/Fontana, 1976. (ISBN: 0564 003018 for the Bible Society) (ISBN: 0005126215 for the Collins)

EPILOGUE

The Bible contains metaphors, symbols, and parables which must be deciphered. Though, the history of the Jewish people in the old testament of the Bible is the main theme of the biblical narrative and sheds light on the intention of the Holy God and His plan for mankind. In the last 5000 years, more than two hundred empires have risen and fallen, and races of men have disappeared from the pages of history, but the Jewish people and their history have survived despite extreme hardship and numerous persecutions. After 1700 years of diaspora and pogrom, the Jews returned to Palestine to form a nation. This event changed the make-up of the Middle East for ever. The historic events in the last 200 to 300 years which led to the creation of the State of Israel are truly amazing. Two major empires, the British and American Empires, rose to gain global power to facilitate the creation of the Israeli State. The British Empire was the mother and the American Empire the father of the State of Israel. The State of Israel finally came of age and became a very powerful country in the Middle East. The advent of globalisation coupled with the legacies of these two empires have fermented a condition which favours further growth and strengthening of the State of Israel. All the indications are that in a not a distant future, Israel will emerge as a major global Judaic Empire, dominating the world in the end times in accordance with the biblical prophesies. The historic events in the West which led to the creation of the State of Israel are fascinating and should be re-visited.

AFTERWORD

The historic events which led to the expulsion of the Jews from the Holy Land by the Romans, their diaspora and subsequent persecution by the Papacy, and the birth of the Zionist movement merit further examination. The Christianisation of the pagan Roman Empire was a turning point in the West and had a profound effect on the destiny of the Jews and the gentiles alike. The rise of the British Empire and its contribution to civilisation is of major importance. The legacy of the Empire and the events and achievements in the last 300 to 350 years include, among many, international commerce, industrial revolution, and creation of a homeland for the Jews. The latter being of huge importance to the fulfilment of the biblical promise of the coming Kingdom of God. God's providence called the British nation to do their duty. The historic events leading to the rise of the American Empire and its relationship with the State of Israel in the Middle East has been crucial in the sustaining of the Jewish State.

Globalisation is playing its role in the fulfilment of the biblical prophesies of the end times. The return of the Jews to Palestine under the British mandate and the building of the third Temple in Jerusalem are decisive events in the modern times in the light of the prophesies in the Bible. There are certain events occurring in the world today which are helping the rise of a Universal Judaic Empire. The rise of a Judaic Empire will end the human experiment and existence in its current form on the earth. The metamorphosis of the State of Israel in the British Empire until its birth in the Middle East in 1946, and the role which the American Empire has been playing in supporting the Jewish State are the key events in the 19th and 20th centuries. The Divine providence called the English-speaking nations to do their historic duty. The events that are now unfolding in the Middle East will take the history to its forgone conclusion and mankind will soon face the judgement seat of Christ. This insight into the biblical prophecy must be shared.

www.ingramcontent.com/pod-product-compliance
Lightning Source LLC
Chambersburg PA
CBHW071540080526
44588CB00011B/1737